To

lov

Sho xxxx

Xmas 2018 ♡

THE GIFT OF
HAPPINESS

YVETTE JANE

summersdale

THE GIFT OF HAPPINESS

Summersdale Publishers Ltd
46 West Street
Chichester
West Sussex
PO19 1RP
UK

www.summersdale.com

Printed and bound in the Czech Republic

ISBN: 978-1-84953-606-6

Substantial discounts on bulk quantities of Summersdale books are available to corporations, professional associations and other organisations. For details contact general enquiries: telephone: +44 (0) 1243 771107, fax: +44 (0) 1243 786300 or email: enquiries@summersdale.com.

TO..

FROM..

Happiness is perhaps best understood as a state of mind.

How we perceive things is a personal choice. By shifting our thoughts to the present moment, past regrets and future worries are discarded, and every experience has the possibility of happiness.

Happy moments can be found in the simplest things closest to home; you may be quietly curled up on the sofa reading a book or pottering about your kitchen; bringing your full attention to these actions can help them feel complete and blissful.

This book is a signpost, pointing the way towards the gift of happiness.

Every day bubbles with possibilities for learning, satisfaction and fun. Be curious about everything!

Avoid grumbling as much
as you can. It becomes a
habit and may spread
like wildfire.

Be appreciative of the things others do for you. Buddhist monks call this 'watering the flowers of gratitude'. Every week, sit down with someone you are close to and tell them all the things you have appreciated about them in the previous days. Let them do the same for you. Practised regularly, this can be a relationship-changer.

Create a 'Happiness Box'. This is your treasure chest, containing pieces of paper on which you have written some moments of happiness. Any time you experience something that has made you smile, filled you with joy, given you immense satisfaction – write it on some paper, fold it up and place in your box. You can then take this out and read through all your moments when you want to boost your happiness levels.

A SMILE IS A
CURVE THAT SETS
EVERYTHING
STRAIGHT.

Phyllis Diller

It really is true – by helping others, we feel happier. It's a great exchange for a little bit of your time each week. Check out your local charities to see how you can get involved and volunteer.

Be flexible and let go of fixed expectations. This gives you the opportunity to embrace whatever comes your way and not regret things turning out differently. *C'est la vie!*

Our bodies produce chemicals called endorphins, which are natural happiness boosters. When you spend time doing something you truly enjoy, your body is flooded with these feel-good chemicals. So try to spend some time on joyful activities every day, from a quiet walk in the country or a park, to an exhilarating cycle ride or run.

Do you have a rainbow of coloured clothes in your wardrobe? Possibly not, but a brightly coloured item of clothing can help you show the world you are happy and full of beans. If you don't have any colourful clothes, make an effort to acquire some!

CHEERFULNESS IS THE VERY FLOWER OF HEALTH.

Proverb

Make time to play! It could be rounders in the garden or tiddlywinks by the fireside. Have good old-fashioned fun and enjoy smiles all round.

Tap into your creativity. Re-imagine an area of your living space or simply decorate or add some new touches to a room in your home; take up a brand new hobby such as watercolour painting, cake decorating or renovating old furniture – anything you feel comfortable with.

The busier we get, the more we put other aspects of our lives on hold. An important contribution to our happiness is the time we spend with close family and good friends, so make the effort and plan a get-together, even if it's just a catch-up cup of tea.

Beware of self-criticism ringing around inside your head. Low levels of self-esteem correlate to lower feelings of happiness, so try to put things into perspective. Build up your sense of appreciation for the positive skills and attributes you possess and recognise the blessings around you in life.

HAPPINESS IS WHEN
WHAT YOU THINK,
WHAT YOU SAY, AND
WHAT YOU DO ARE
IN HARMONY.

Mahatma Gandhi

Change your words and you will change your feelings. Replace, 'I have to do it' with 'I want to do it'. This creates an energetic shift and enables you to feel more empowered. Try it any time you hear yourself thinking 'I have to' or 'I should'.

Let go of heaviness – things don't have to be serious all the time. Lighten up with a joke and try to laugh at life's absurdities.

Animals have been proven to be natural mood enhancers. By spending time with a pet you may see a reduction in your stress levels – and plenty of reasons to laugh and be cheerful! If you don't have a pet, why not pay a visit to a friend or relative who does.

Sit down and plan a trip to a destination you have dreamed of. Even if it may not happen for years, or not at all, it is uplifting and exciting to while away a few hours. Who knows, the dream may eventually become a reality!

HAPPINESS IS NOT A
STATE TO ARRIVE AT,
BUT A MANNER OF
TRAVELLING.

Margaret Lee Runbeck

Smile! It's a simple and quick way to start feeling happy. Give it a try!

It is said in Native American lore that there are two wolves within your heart. You can feed the wolf of love and happiness or the wolf of hate and ill-will – whichever one you feed will grow.

What are you passionate about? What energises you? Which of your friends do you have the most fun with? Recognise how you can choose to lift your spirits by following your heart.

Santosa is a Sanskrit word meaning 'contentment and acceptance for where we are right now'. Allow this beautiful word to enter your vocabulary and let its message brighten your daily life.

SPEAK OR ACT WITH
A PURE MIND AND
HAPPINESS WILL
FOLLOW YOU AS
YOUR SHADOW,
UNSHAKABLE.

Buddha

Set your intention for the day to be happy and kind. You have a choice.

Increase your sense of happiness and well-being by interacting with people who share your interests.

The happiest couples are those who spend time together on enjoyable activities. However busy life becomes, make time to share fun – even if it's just exercising, browsing a farmers' market or watching a film. Staying in touch with and making time for friends is equally valuable.

Slow down and pay attention to your surroundings. Use all your senses to enjoy your current environment, and before moving on, get your next destination clear in your mind.

THE MORE LIGHT YOU
ALLOW WITHIN YOU,
THE BRIGHTER THE
WORLD YOU LIVE
IN WILL BE.

Shakti Gawain

Walking is one of
the most effective ways to
replenish your inner joy, so
incorporate a short walk
into your daily routine
if you can.

High levels of the mineral selenium are found in seafood, seaweed, Brazil nuts and wholegrain cereals. It is essential for brain function and can significantly improve your mood. Eat yourself happy!

When a strong emotion arises – such as anger, hurt or fear – allow yourself to pause before you react. Notice your breath and the sensations in your body. You may then recognise that you have a choice about what you do next.

Think about how you can create more happiness for others. Thinking and planning something special for another person can be as enjoyable and fulfilling as the recipient's experience.

THE FOOLISH MAN
SEEKS HAPPINESS
IN THE DISTANCE,
THE WISE GROWS IT
UNDER HIS FEET.

James Oppenheim

Be joyful, because there is always music.

Find little things that you're good at and allow simplicity to give meaning and purpose to your life. You don't have to strive to be the world's greatest at anything in order to be happy – doing everything to the best of your ability is enough!

Start each day with a positive morning routine. Allow yourself time for meditation (or at least a moment of reflection), a healthy breakfast and some exercise. You can then move into your day calm and happy.

Keep some of your favourite pieces of writing close to hand, so that you can refer to them when you feel yourself slipping towards negativity. Poems, prayers, song lyrics or phrases from a favourite novel can all replenish and inspire.

FOLKS ARE USUALLY ABOUT AS HAPPY AS THEY MAKE UP THEIR MINDS TO BE.

Abraham Lincoln

A hug can be a great
happiness-booster.

Give yourself happy feet
by joining a dance class:
ballroom, flamenco, salsa,
swing – anything that
takes your fancy!

Love the place you live. Sometimes being away from home reminds us of how fond of it we really are. Look with renewed eyes on your home and appreciate everything your area has to offer.

Try an internal smile – think of something happy and wonderful and experience the warm smiling feeling within. You can tap into this internal smile whenever you wish.

A TABLE, A CHAIR, A BOWL OF FRUIT AND A VIOLIN; WHAT ELSE DOES A MAN NEED TO BE HAPPY?

Albert Einstein

Research shows that our happiness not only flourishes with those in our direct social network, such as neighbours, friends and family, but is influenced by the people our friends know too. So joyfulness echoes out through groups of people, like a radar system. Keep in contact and spread the joy!

Sometimes we need to make time to be in awe of life. Stand on the top of a mountain or hill, or look up at an expanse of night sky in the wilderness. Happiness comes from our sense of not being separate from one another or from nature.

Never feel guilty about spending your time reading a good book. Relish every moment as you are transported to a completely different world within the pages, and are inspired by the myriad experiences of humanity.

Create a 'vision board' collage which depicts what goals and priorities you want to fulfil in your life. Keep your vision board in view so that you can frequently look at it and remind yourself of the happy direction your life is taking.

Do one thing at a time with
concentration and joy.

Accept the things in life that you can't change and focus on achieving the goals that are possible for you.

MODERATION. SMALL
HELPINGS. SAMPLE
A LITTLE BIT OF
EVERYTHING. THESE
ARE THE SECRETS OF
HAPPINESS AND
GOOD HEALTH.

Julia Child

A simple way of increasing your happiness levels is to place a vase of flowers in your home or workplace if allowed. Each time you glance at them, enjoy how you feel uplifted and glad.

If you are redecorating the walls of your home, consider the best colours that elicit a happy response for you. Everyone has different tastes, so choose colours that are calming, yet uplifting. As a result you will feel more positive about returning home to your joyful surroundings.

BE IN LOVE WITH YOUR LIFE, EVERY DETAIL OF IT.

Jack Kerouac

If you experience the noise of negative chatter in your mind, remember that it is a sign you need to attune to a positive, happier state. You have the capacity to do this by sitting still and listening to the inner wisdom that resides within you. Don't buy in to the myth of your inadequacy.

Keep learning! It develops your curiosity, teaches you new skills, introduces you to new friends and, best of all, it contributes to feelings of happiness.

Take time to unplug from technology. If you're waiting in a queue, resist the urge to check texts and emails on your phone. Take notice of your posture and adjust it to be comfortable. Focus on your breathing while you wait, remaining calm and undisturbed.

Feeling a little under the weather? Try some 'joy breathing'. Recall a memory when you felt happy. Allow that joyful experience to flow all around your body like a warming sun. Breathe slowly, filling every cell with contented bliss.

Optimism is, largely, better for your welfare than pessimism. It can make you more enjoyable company too!

Always be happy for
the success of others –
be generous with your
congratulations and the
joy will spread.

IF YOU HAVE A GARDEN
AND A LIBRARY, YOU
HAVE EVERYTHING
YOU NEED.

Cicero

As we get older we grow happier. With maturing years we better appreciate the true value of family and friends, which makes us feel more content. Our brains also contain increased levels of the chemicals that enable us to feel stable and sanguine. Let's raise a toast to our elder years!

Have you noticed that when you feel in a low mood you may have intense cravings for foods containing refined sugar, like chocolate and cake? This is your body's way of getting a quick fix of happiness, because eating sugar produces insulin which elicits a temporary feeling of elation. Better food choices to improve your mood would be those rich in vitamin B6, such as spinach and salmon, and magnesium-rich foods like bananas and oat bran.

IF YOU WANT
YOUR LIFE TO BE A
MAGNIFICENT STORY,
THEN BEGIN BY
REALISING THAT YOU
ARE THE AUTHOR.

Mark Houlahan

Be clear about what motivates you. High achievers have been found to have a strong desire to achieve, whereas those less accomplished simply wish to avoid failure. You can view demanding tasks as needing dedication and commitment, rather than as overloading and stressful. It's your choice!

Sometimes chores remain in the back of our minds, waiting to get done. It could be checking out prices of electricity suppliers, renewing a magazine subscription or making an overdue dental appointment. For an instant happiness rush, deal with it now.

Memorise a good joke so
you can bring it to mind in
a moment of dullness.

Put out bird seed and a bird bath to encourage feathered friends to visit you. Their antics can be a marvellous tonic.

Consider joining in with community events, local clubs and other group activities in your town. A sense of belonging is one of the keys to happiness.

Be happy with the
person you are and all
your relationships will
be healthy.

AT THE HEIGHT
OF LAUGHTER, THE
UNIVERSE IS FLUNG
INTO A KALEIDOSCOPE
OF NEW POSSIBILITIES.

Jean Houston

Get close to nature and go camping. Experience sunrises, cockerel wake-up calls and cooking over a stove in the open air – all things that will make you feel glad to be alive!

As you tidy up around the house, sing loudly – or whistle – with exuberance.

HAPPINESS ARISES IN A STATE OF PEACE, NOT A STATE OF TUMULT.

Ann Radcliffe

Give up the search for happiness. Looking for something means you have placed it outside yourself. Seek out joy by listening to the inner voice of your heart.

Learn to meditate. Regular practise instils changes in the brain that reprogram its structure, guiding you to a calmer, contented and happier state of mind.

Spend some time with children. If you don't have your own children, visit nieces and nephews or other young family members, and enjoy the sheer exuberance that they bring to the simplest of things.

Sometimes it feels like pure bliss to soak in a hot, bubbly bath. Have a glass of your favourite tipple and light a candle to increase the feeling of happiness.

Spending your money on 'experiences' – like eating out and travelling to new or favourite places – rather than on expensive items can be very rewarding. Research indicates we glean more happiness from our memories than from material things, so consider this next time you reach for your purse or wallet.

Be mindful of building up your expectations – this can lead to dissatisfaction when things don't go to plan. Keep an unruffled and placid approach and gentle contentment will follow.

HAPPINESS IS
NOT A GOAL... IT'S
A BY-PRODUCT OF A
LIFE WELL LIVED.

Eleanor Roosevelt

Clear a shelf or a corner of your house and transform it into an area of peace with natural items such as shells, crystals or driftwood.

Don't compare yourself
to others, especially those
in the media who are not
representative of real life.
You are unique, so stay
optimistic and positive.

BE CONTENT WITH
WHAT YOU HAVE;
REJOICE IN THE WAY
THINGS ARE. WHEN
YOU REALISE THERE IS
NOTHING LACKING,
THE WHOLE WORLD
BELONGS TO YOU.

Lao Tzu

Celebrate! There are many opportunities, outside of birthdays, to share happiness and gratitude: the completion of a big work project, the all-clear with a health issue, the start of something new. All of life's stepping stones deserve joyful acknowledgement.

The word 'resilience' stems from the Latin *resilio*, meaning 'to jump back'. In our everyday lives we need to find ways of bouncing back from adversity, to pick ourselves up and carry on. Having supportive friends and managing our behaviour positively are two helpful resilience strategies.

Keep photos of loved ones nearby so you can glance at them and feel a sense of joy.

Simple pleasures can bring a great deal of inner contentment. Return to a favourite place for a leisurely browse – a bookshop, a library or an antique centre.

The meaning of life is not a search but a choice made by you. Every moment of your day you can interpret events and choose what meaning to place on them.

Train yourself to be happy and fulfilled by looking for the positive things around you. When new developments occur in your life, you will then be open to the possibilities they bring, rather than focusing on the problems.

TRUE HAPPINESS IS
AN INNER POWER –
NATURAL, HEALING,
ABUNDANT AND
ALWAYS AVAILABLE.

Robert Holden

Be content in this moment with whatever you are doing.

Remember to have patience.
Things come to fruition at
the right time.

HAPPINESS DEPENDS UPON OURSELVES.

Aristotle

Do you remember how things seemed magical when you were a child? Look out for moments of enchantment, courtesy of nature: a rainbow, shimmering raindrops on tree branches or a bird singing. Allow yourself to cherish these glimpses of wonder in your heart.

Your brain reacts in the same way whether you are experiencing something that makes you feel happy or just thinking about something happy – both can flood your body with feel-good hormones. This means that you can influence how you feel by what you choose to think. So think happy!

Telling people about good events increases our day-to-day happiness, over and above the beneficial effects of those good things happening.

When we look at ourselves without judgement we can experience a richness of being that contains true happiness and love.

Increase your feelings of peace and calm by wearing flowing, naturally-made clothes in light colours. White, yellow, pale pink or blue can enhance softness and gentleness as you float butterfly-like through your day.

Weekends can often be as stressful as working weekdays. Plan one day for chores and the other for having fun with family, or whatever brings you happiness.

HAPPINESS COMES
WHEN YOUR WORK
AND WORDS ARE OF
BENEFIT TO YOURSELF
AND OTHERS.

Jack Kornfield

Look up at the stars
and make a wish on
one of them.

Consciously look for the
beauty, positivity and
love in your life.

LAUGHTER IS AN INSTANT VACATION.

Milton Berle

Remember the dreams you had as a child to travel the world, work with horses or be an actor? If those dreams have not been fulfilled, visualise what passions still remain. How could you manifest a part of your dream into your current life? Perhaps book a trip abroad, go for a horse ride along the seashore or sign up with your local amateur dramatic society.

If you find yourself excessively worrying about things, it may be worth trying some cognitive behavioural therapy (CBT). This is a brief, one-to-one treatment to help you notice when you are worrying, break the habit and then implement alternative ways of reacting to your everyday problems.

Consider reducing your intake of negative news. Politics, wars and economic fluctuations can be overwhelming and gloomy so, without disconnecting altogether, remember to take a break from the Internet, TV and radio.

Learn to live with loose ends. You may be decorating your home, making a dress, reading a book – enjoy the process. Your happiness is not on hold until the project is completed.

Share your own happiness by sending joyful thoughts to someone who is feeling sad or unwell today. Simply bring them to mind and imagine you are directing loving wishes towards them, to arrive even faster than special delivery.

Many people are now choosing happiness by developing a 'lifestyle business'. This is where you work on something you are passionate about, and is location-independent with flexible hours. It can be started alongside your paid job and quite often works well with child-rearing. So be creative and think outside the box to manifest the life–work balance that you really want.

THE GREATEST
HAPPINESS IS TO
TRANSFORM ONE'S
FEELINGS INTO
ACTION.

Madame de Staël

Smile and say hello to a stranger. The worst thing they can do is ignore you; the best is that you may have cheered them up.

Focus on your own achievements rather than comparing yourself to others. This is the best way to nurture your own happiness and self-esteem.

WEALTH CONSISTS
NOT IN HAVING GREAT
POSSESSIONS, BUT IN
HAVING FEW WANTS.

Epictetus

Create an 'action list'. Place on it things you have been meaning to try, future goals for your work and ideas for spending time with friends and family. Look over it now and again to remind you of life's possibilities and to nudge you into new directions.

Do you find yourself thinking things like, 'I'm not clever enough' or 'I'm never going to be good at this'? If so, it's time to press the delete button on negative self-talk and replace it with positive. Write down some inspiring phrases and read them to yourself daily.

Move from small talk to deeper conversations with friends. It's good to connect with people and share ideas. Bonding with others is one of the core factors for happiness.

Strive for perfection
and you may well
never be happy.

Seasonal Affective Disorder (SAD) affects many people in the winter, when they feel tired and glum. You can boost your levels of happiness and sunshine by using a daylight therapy lamp (light box), which are readily available from many outlets.

Return the spring to your step by delegating tasks to others in all areas of your life. This means more teamwork and being willing to relinquish control, relieving pressure on you.

ALL THE HAPPINESS
THERE IS IN THIS
WORLD ARISES FROM
WISHING OTHERS
TO BE HAPPY.

Geshe Kelsang Gyatso

Raise your activity level right now – run up the stairs, stand up if you are on the telephone, take a walk round the office or, for an extra boost, pop outside for a brisk 5-minute walk.

A sign of your happiness at work is whether you take the initiative in things. Being creative, making suggestions and doing additional tasks are all ways to make work feel more satisfying.

GO CONFIDENTLY
IN THE DIRECTION
OF YOUR DREAMS.
LIVE THE LIFE YOU'VE
IMAGINED.

Henry David Thoreau

Savour the everyday things that you enjoy. Focus on anything you like – hugging your pet, drinking a refreshing juice or smelling the food you are about to eat. Give yourself time to notice these agreeable things and life becomes full of plentiful small pleasures.

Humans have over 60,000 thoughts a day. We can't change what we are feeling but we can alter our reactions to our thoughts. This means becoming conscious of what we are thinking, identifying the thought and realising that it need not dictate our lives. We can observe our thoughts and feelings, let them go and carry on.

Look for happiness and
you will find it!